INTRODUCING THE STAR OF THIS BOOK

★ **DIPLODOCUS** ★

(dI-PLOD-Oh-KUSS)

DID YOU KNOW...

that *Diplodocus* is one of the longest dinosaurs ever to have lived. It's also one of the best known, as several nearly complete skeletons have been discovered!

Diplodocus means 'double beam'

SETTING THE SCENE

It all started around 231 million years ago (mya), when the first dinosaurs appeared, part-way through the Triassic Period.

The Age of the Dinosaurs had begun, a time when dinosaurs ruled the world!

Scientists call this time the

MESOZOIC ERA
(mez-oh-zoh-ic)

and this era was so long that they divided it into three periods.

TRIASSIC
lasted 51 million years

JURASSIC
lasted 56 million years

252 million years ago

201 million years ago

Diplodocus lived during the Jurassic Period from 154 – 150 million years ago.

CRETACEOUS
lasted 79 million years

145 million years ago   66 million years ago

WEATHER REPORT

The world didn't always look like it does today. Before the dinosaurs, and during the early part of the Mesozoic Era, the land was all stuck together in one supercontinent called Pangaea. Over time, things changed and by the end of the Jurassic Period the land looked like this.

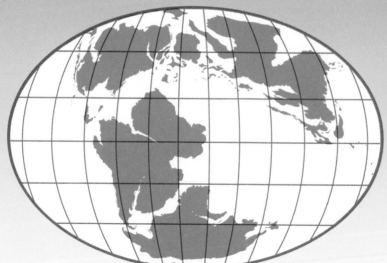

JURASSIC 150 mya
Named after the Jura Mountains in the European Alps

TRIASSIC

Very hot, dry and dusty

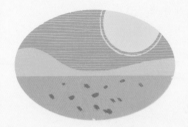

JURASSIC

Hot, humid and tropical

CRETACEOUS

Warm, wet and seasonal

As the land split apart, more coastlines appeared. The weather changed from dry to humid and many of the deserts changed into lush rain forests.

HOMETOWN

Here's what's been discovered so far and where...

COLORADO

USA

PALAEONTOLOGIST
OTHNIEL CHARLES MARSH
NAMED DIPLODOCUS
IN 1878

Several partial skeletons,
one almost complete.

The very first *Diplodocus* bones were discovered in a quarry near Canon City,
Colorado, USA, by Benjamin Mudge and Samuel Williston in 1877. Since then
other bones have been found elsewhere in the USA.

Two species of *Diplodocus* are identified today and the most complete is
Diplodocus carnegii, named after Scottish-American steel magnate, Andrew
Carnegie. Mr Carnegie had 11 replicas made which he donated to several
countries, making *Diplodocus* one of the most displayed dinosaurs in the world!

VITAL STATISTICS

During the Jurassic Period plant life became more varied, so there was plenty for the herbivores (plant-eating dinosaurs) to eat. As a result, they got bigger and bigger and *Diplodocus* was a true giant of its time!

Let's look at *Diplodocus* and see what's special, quirky and downright amazing about this dinosaur!

DIPLODOCUS

5m high from toe to hip

This Jurassic giant was too big to fit through your front door. It would need three doors on top of each other, and at least six next to each other, if it wanted to get in!

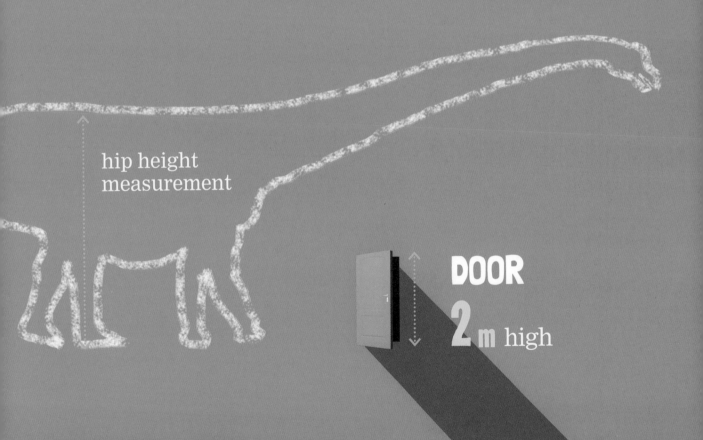

hip height measurement

DOOR

2m high

DIPLODOCUS

Length: up to 26 m

Height: 5 m from toe to hip

Weight: 10 – 15 tonnes

BUS Traditional double decker

Length: 11 m   **Height:** 4.5 m   **Weight:** 8 tonnes (empty)

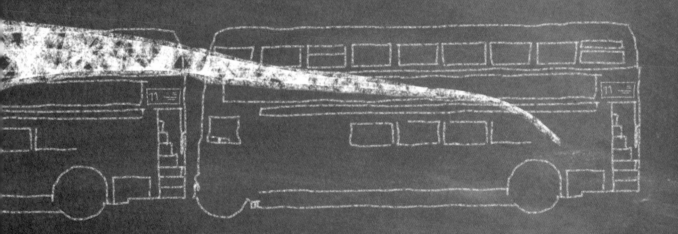

MOUSE

SCARY SCALE

How does *Diplodocus* rate?

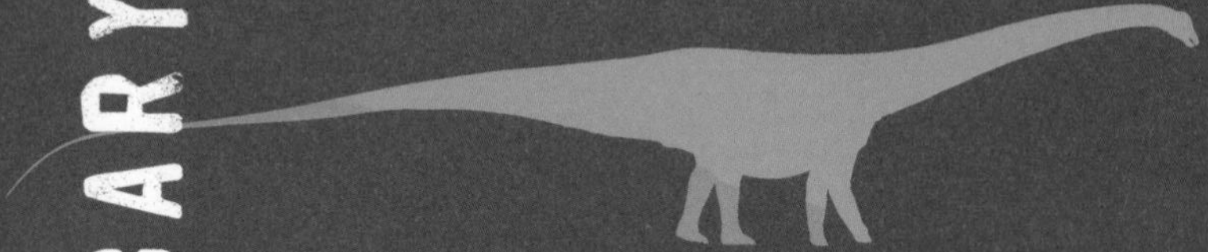

NOT SCARY

1 2 3 4 5

↑ Whilst wandering around and eating.

When under attack.
An attacking dinosaur
would have to watch
out for the *Diplodocus*
whip-like tail which
was a lethal weapon…
More later!

6 7 8 9 10

BRAININESS

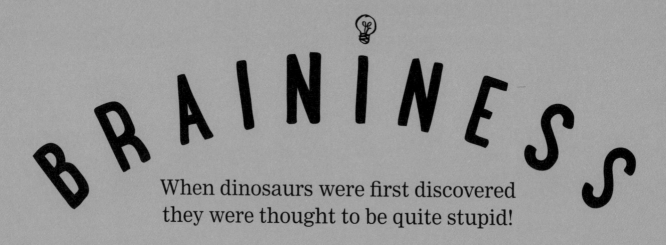

When dinosaurs were first discovered
they were thought to be quite stupid!

Then a few scientists thought that some dinosaurs had
a second brain close to their butt! That's now just a myth.

Today scientists know that dinosaurs had one brain and were
intelligent for reptiles. Some were among the most intelligent
creatures alive during the Mesozoic Era, although
still not as smart as most modern mammals.

By looking at the:

Body size

Size of the brain

Sense of smell

Eyesight

scientists can tell how they rated against each other...

WHERE DOES DIPLODOCUS, A PLANT-EATING DINOSAUR, STAND ON THE 'BRAINY SCALE'?

TROODON
(TRU-oh-don)

10/10
CARNIVORE
(brainiest)

T. REX
(tie-RAN-oh-SAW-russ rex)

9/10
CARNIVORE

IGUANODON
(ig-WAHN-oh-DON)

6/10
HERBIVORE

STEGOSAURUS
(STEG-oh-SAW-russ)

4/10
HERBIVORE

ANKYLOSAURUS
(an-KIE-loh-SAW-russ)

3/10
HERBIVORE

DIPLODOCUS
(di-PLOD-oh-KUSS)

2/10
HERBIVORE
(not so brainy)

These dinosaurs are drawn to scale in relation to each other!

SPEED O METER

SLOW

1 2 3 4 5

Diplodocus was a sauropod: a huge four-legged herbivore, with a long neck and tail, small head and massive limbs. Some estimates suggest that sauropods like *Diplodocus* may have reached top speeds of around 12 – 15 mph.

6 7 8 9 10

FAST

WEAPONS

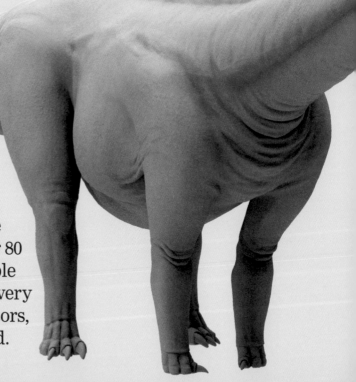

6/10

Even though a fully grown adult had little to fear from hungry carnivores, it still needed to be able to defend the younger or older members of the herd. Apart from its size, the one weapon that a *Diplodocus* had was its tail...

TAIL

At 14 – 15 m long, the tail made up more than half of the length of a *Diplodocus*. With over 80 vertebrae, the tail was very supple and could have been whipped out very fast to lash out at potential predators, creating a loud 'cracking' sound.

BRAIN

Its tiny brain was about the size of a child's fist, typically small for a large herbivore in comparison to its body.

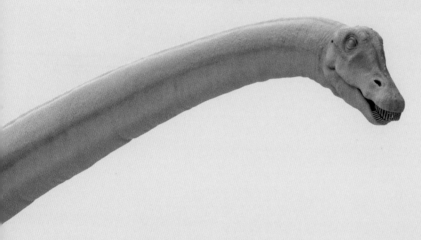

NECK

The neck was 7 m or more and was made up of 15 elongated vertebrae (back and neck bones). It was heavy and stiff and scientists think that a *Diplodocus* wouldn't have been able to raise it much higher than horizontal.

HEART

Diplodocus required a huge heart to pump blood around such a large body. It has been estimated that the heart may have weighed around 1.5 tonnes, about the weight of a small car!

TEETH

With forward-pointing, peg-like teeth that were bunched at the front of its mouth, the teeth of a *Diplodocus* were perfect branch-strippers. *Diplodocus* fed by closing its mouth around the stems and stripping the leaves by pulling back its head – like a rake.

This process would wear the teeth down, but it was no problem for a *Diplodocus*, as its teeth were continually replaced throughout its life.

As it didn't have any back teeth *Diplodocus* couldn't grind up its food, so it had to swallow it whole.

12 cm

Tooth to scale:

12 CM FROM ROOT TO TIP

DIET

Scientists now agree that the neck of a *Diplodocus* was too heavy and stiff to lift past horizontal whilst feeding, so it would have eaten low and medium-lying plants such as ginkgoes, seed ferns, cycads, club mosses and horsetails.

It is likely that *Diplodocus* could have reared up on its hind legs for a long time, with its tail acting as a third support, enabling it to reach up and eat the lush leaves at the tops of the trees!

Like several dinosaurs, *Diplodocus* swallowed pebbles called gastroliths, which rolled around in their stomachs, helping to break down the tough plants.

WHO LIVED IN THE SAME
NEIGHBOURHOOD?

TORVOSAURUS
(TOR-vo-SAW-russ)

This 9 m long, 2 tonne carnivorous theropod (walked on two legs) could have been a real threat to a young or old *Diplodocus*. Along with *Allosaurus*, it would have been a vicious predator (an animal that hunts other animals). There has never been a complete skeleton found, so it may have been much bigger.

ALLOSAURUS
(AL-oh-SAW-russ)

At 9 m in length and weighing 1.5 tonnes, a lone *Allosaurus* was not much of a threat to an adult *Diplodocus*, but a young, old or weak *Diplodocus* would be an easier target, especially if the *Allosaurus* was hunting in a pack. It is likely that adult *Diplodocus* used their whip-like tails to scare off these predators.

WHICH ANIMAL ALIVE TODAY IS MOST LIKE DIPLODOCUS?

You have learnt how important the neck and tail were to a *Diplodocus*. There are several animals alive today that also rely on these features.

Giraffes take advantage of their long necks by reaching up high to grasp the leaves and strip branches from the tops of the trees, as well as looking imposing and intimidating.

Horses, cows and zebras
are examples of animals
that whip out their tails to
swat away annoying flies.

WHAT'S SO SPECIAL ABOUT DIPLODOCUS?

WHEN DIPLODOCUS LIVED

JURASSIC 154 - 150 mya

TOOTH SIZE

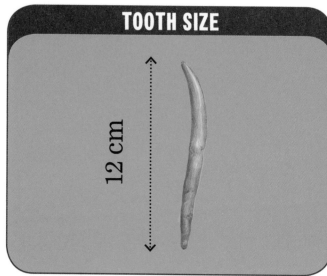

12 cm

WEIGHT

15 TONNES

FAST OR SLOW?

SPEED
out of 10

4

THE BEST BITS!

DISCOVERED, SO FAR

SEVERAL NEARLY COMPLETE SKELETONS

HOW FRIGHTENING?

SCARY

2	6
if chilling	if attacked

MEAT OR PLANTS?

SPECIAL BITS

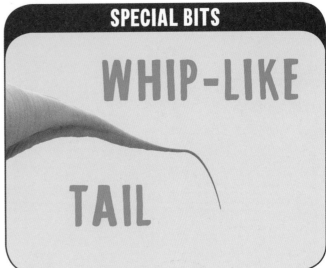

WHIP-LIKE TAIL

WHAT'S NEXT ?

OTHER EXCITING TITLES AVAILABLE NOW!

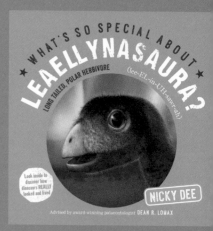

TRICERATOPS
last and largest of the horned dinosaurs

MEGALOSAURUS
the first to be named

LEAELLYNASAURA
long tailed, polar herbivore

COMING SOON

Velociraptor
turkey-sized, feathered pack-hunter

Spinosaurus
large, semi-aquatic, fish-eater

Brachiosaurus
heavy, giraffe-like giant

Maiasaura
motherly, duck-billed herbivore

Join the 'What's So Special Club'

JOIN OUR FREE CLUB

 Download fun dinosaur quizzes and colouring-in sheets
www.specialdinosaurs.com

 Enter the exciting world of a 3D artist and discover
how a 3D dinosaur is created and made to look real!

 Find out more about our experts and when they
first became fascinated by dinosaurs.

 Who is Nicky Dee? Meet the author online.

 Join the club and be the first to hear about
exciting new books, activities and games.

 Club members will be first in line to order
new books in the series!

COPYRIGHT

Copyright Published in 2016
by The Dragonfly Group Ltd

info@specialdinosaurs.com
www.specialdinosaurs.com

First printed in 2016
Copyright © Nicky Dee 2016
Nicky Dee has asserted her right under the
Copyright, Designs, and Patents Act 1988 to be
identified as the Author of this work.

A catalogue record for this book is available
from the British Library.

ISBN: 978-0-9935293-4-4

Printed in China

ACKNOWLEDGEMENTS

Dean R. Lomax
talented, multiple award-winning
palaeontologist, author and science
communicator and the consultant
for the series   www.deanrlomax.co.uk

David Eldridge and The Curved House
for original book design and artworking

Gary Hanna
thoroughly talented 3D artist

Scott Hartman
skeletons and silhouettes, professional
palaeoartist and palaeontologist

Ian Durneen
skilled digital sketch artist of the
guest dinosaurs

Ron Blakey
Colorado Plateau Geosystems Inc.
creator of the original
paleogeographic maps

My family
patient, encouraging and wonderfully
supportive. Thank you!

To find out more about our artists, designers
and illustrators please visit the website
www.specialdinosaurs.com